George W. Carleton

Our Artist in Peru

George W. Carleton

Our Artist in Peru

ISBN/EAN: 9783337258511

Printed in Europe, USA, Canada, Australia, Japan

Cover: Foto ©Andreas Hilbeck / pixelio.de

More available books at **www.hansebooks.com**

OUR

ARTIST IN PERU.

[FIFTY DRAWINGS ON WOOD.]

LEAVES FROM
THE SKETCH-BOOK OF A TRAVELLER,
DURING THE WINTER OF 1865-6,

BY

GEO. W. CARLETON,
Author of " Our Artist in Cuba," etc.

" Let observation, with expansive view,
Survey mankind from China to Peru."

NEW YORK:
Carleton, Publisher, 413 *Broadway.*
London: S Low Son & Co.
MDCCCLXVI.

J. P. Davis & Speer, Engravers and Printers.

CONTENTS.

A Preliminary Word.

A PRELIMINARY WORD.

THE flattering reception that last year attended the publication of *Our Artist in Cuba*, has led its author to issue this little book of a similar character, which shadows forth such trifling but novel incidents as helped to gild many odd moments during a recent pleasure-trip to Peru.

No attempt is made to voluminously describe the sad sea (sicky) waves of the Atlantic ocean in the stormy month of February— nor the sunny view of Cuba, as you pass its eastern cocoa-wooded point—nor that tempest in a teapot, the Carib Sea—nor pandemonium broke loose, the town of Aspinwall, with negroes thick like leaves of Vallambrosa, only not nearly so sweet-scented—nor that miracle of engineering skill, the Panama Railroad, which intoxicates the susceptive traveller with its wild scenery and its parasitical fringe of tropical vegetation—nor strange, old, Spanish Panama, with its huge ecclesiastical ruins, its Barber-of-Seville sort of streets, and its everlastingly crowing game-cocks—nor that hottest of little islands, Taboga, from whose tranquil

bay the English steamers start on their south-
ward trips—nor the voyage down the Pacific,
with vessel so comfortable, sea so smooth,
and weather so chief among ten thousand,
and altogether lovely—nor the curious little
seaports at intervals on the coast, with their
wild Indian populations, and their zoological
and pomological surprises—nor the arrival at
Callao, where one utters an *Ave Maria* each
night, if he hasn't been earthquaked during
the day—nor Lima *itself*, that South Ameri-
can paradise, which to describe would be to
bewilder Scheherazade with all her imagina-
tion.

These things, and many, many more, does
the pocket note-book of Our Artist retain
little sketchy impressions of—and essaying
only to convey a ray of information through
the glasses of humor, the Author has multi-
plied with printers'-ink his book of sketches,
which, although caricatures, are but exaggera-
tions of actual events, on the spur of the
moment jotted down, for the same sort of
mere pastime as may lead the reader to linger
along its ephemeral pages.

NEW YORK, July, 1866.

THE START—STEAMSHIP "HENRY CHAUNCEY,"
FROM NEW YORK TO ASPINWALL.

Sea-sickness being a weakness of Our Artist, he determines to be fore-armed, and accordingly provides himself with a few simple preventives, warmly recommended by his various friends.

IN THE CARIBBEAN SEA.

Our Artist, having indulged rather freely in the different preventives, gets things mixed, and wishes that his friends and their confounded antidotes were at the bottom of the Dead Sea.

ARRIVAL AT ASPINWALL.

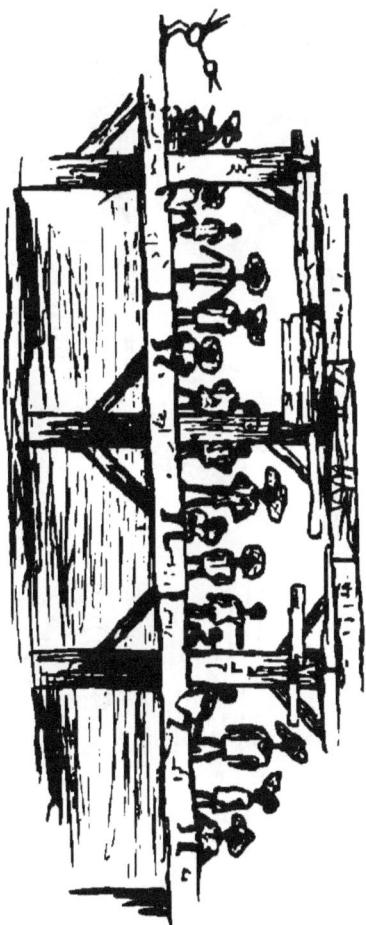

First impressions of the city and its inhabitants—Colored citizens on the dock, awaiting the steamer's advent.

ISTHMUS OF DARIEN.

View from the window of a Panama railroad car—showing the low-neck and short-sleeve style of costume adopted by the youthful natives of Cruces,—Also a sprightly specimen of the one-eared greyhound indigenous to the country.

4

A VIEW IN PANAMA.

The old and weather-beaten church of Santa Ana—and in the foreground, with basket on her head, baby under one arm, and bowl of milk supported by the other, a colored lady of West Indian descent, vulgarly known as a "Jamaica nigger."

5

Deeming it always incumbent upon the traveller to invest in the products of the country, Our Artist provides himself with a good sensible Panama hat, and thus with wife and "mutual friend," he peacefully and serenely meanders around among the suburbs of the city.

A STREET SCENE IN PANAMA.

Our Artist, with the naked eye, beholds a pig, a fighting-cock, and a black baby, all tied by the leg, at the humble doorway of the residence of a colored citizen, in the principal street of the capital of Central America.

7

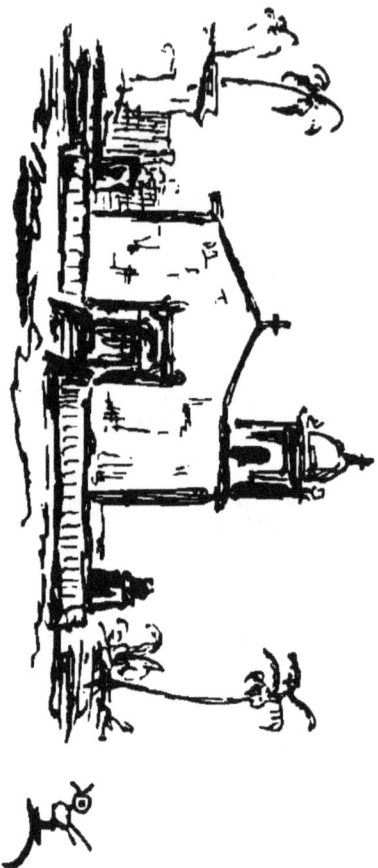

Our Artist wanders about the sleepy little neighboring island, Taboga, where the English steamers lie, and sketches, among other picturesque bits, the clean little whitewashed cathedral in the dirty little Broadway of Taboga.

STEAMSHIP "CHILE."
FROM PANAMA TO CALLAO.

Crossing the equinoctial line, Our Artist discovers that the rays of a vertical sun are anything but bracing and cool.

PAYTA—A SEAPORT IN PERU.

Our Artist, having understood that this town is chiefly remarkable for its fine breed of mules, ironically inquires of a native Venus if this can be considered a good specimen. The N. V. treats Our Artist with silent, stolid, Indian contempt.

10

NATURAL HISTORY IN PERU.

Our Artist visits a coasting-vessel just arrived from Guayaquil, loaded with every variety of tropical fruit, and a sprinkling of tame monkeys, parrots, alligators, white herons, iguanas, paroquets, spotted deer, etc.

ARRIVAL AT CALLAO—THE HARBOR.

The landing-boat being a trifle too much loaded by the head, Our Artist finds it somewhat difficult to steer.

12

ARCHITECTURE IN CALLAO.

The little one-story Cathedral on the Plaza, which the earthquakes have so frantically and so vainly tried to swallow up or tumble down.

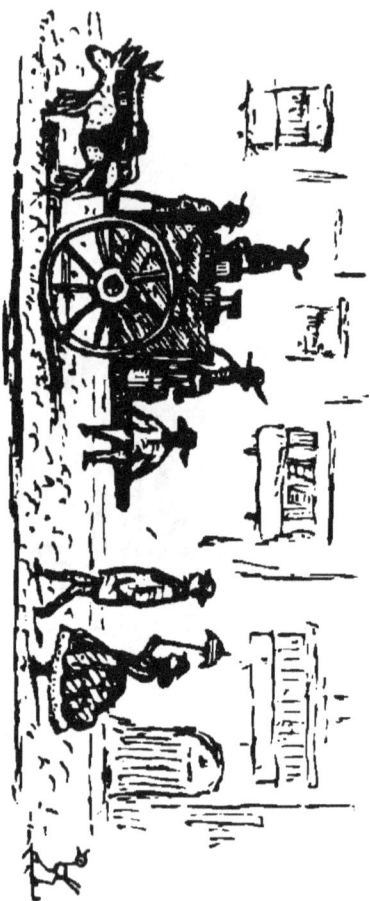

Triumphal entry of Our Artist and his much-the-better-half; reviving the brilliant days of Pizarro and his conquering warriors, as they entered the "City of the Kings."—The Peruvian warriors in the present century, however, conquer but the baggage, and permit the weary traveller to walk to his hotel at the tail-end of the procession.

14

THE CATHEDRAL AT LIMA.

An after-dinner sketch (rather shaky) from our balcony in the Hotel Morin, on the Grand Plaza.

One of the waiters at our hotel, clad in the inevitable *poncho* --A genuine native Peruvian, perhaps a son of "Rolla the Peruvian," who was "within."

Peeping into the kitchen one day, Our Artist perceives that a costume, cool and negligé, may be improvised by making a hole in a coffee-bag and getting into it.

STREETS OF LIMA—CALLE JUDIOS.

Almost every other street in Lima has a stream of filthy water or open sewer running through the middle of it, offering rich fishing-grounds to the graceful *gallinazos* or turkey-buzzards, who thus constitute the street-cleaning department of the municipal government.

18

CELESTIALS IN PERU.

Our Artist is here seen resisting the tempting offer of a bowl of what appears to be buzzard soup, in front of one of the Chinese cook-shops that abound in the neighborhood of the market at Lima.

19

DOLCE FAR NIENTE—A DREAM OF PERÚ.

Our Artist before going to Lima, during little poetical siestas, had indulged in lovely romantic reveries, the burden of which he sketches in his mind's eye, Horatio—but

Alas! too frequently his thirsty eye is met only by such
visions as the above—and the lovely beauties of Lima, where
are they?

BEDROOMS IN PERU.

A section of the inner-wall to our chamber at the Hotel in Lima.—The condition of things at the witching hour of night, judging by the sounds.

A young **Peruvian** accompanying its mamma to market in
the morning.

A picturesque little *mirador* or lookout at the corner of
Calle Plateros and Bodegones, opposite the Hotel Maury,
with balconies *ad lib.*

The *panadero*, or baker, as he appears on his mite of a donkey, rushing round through the streets of Lima, delivering bread to his customers.

25

Our Artist, after a hearty dinner, extravagantly engages a three-horse coupé, and goes out for a regular, genuine, native Peruvian ride.

That his bones are unbroken, and that he is yet alive to tell the tale, remains to him an unfathomable mystery.

Our Artist has heard a good deal about the magnificent eyes of the Limanian women ; but as he never sees more than one eye at a time, he can't say much about them, with any regard for the truth.

The Señoritas look very prettily sometimes, with their black mantillas thrown gracefully over their heads, (*See Geographies, etc.*,) but when you come across a party possessing a decided nose, in profile, the effect is rather startling.

Our apartments look out upon the Grand Plaza, where the fighting usually takes place ; and as the windows are mostly broken by the balls of the last Revolution, (Nov. 6, 1865,) and it's about time for another, Our Artist gets into ambuscade every time he hears a fire-cracker in the street.

Two native and dreadfully patriotic Peruvian soldiers on review before their superior officer.

The National Hymn, with variations, as rendered by the Royal Band in front of President Prado's palace on the Grand Plaza.

31

A hasty sketch of Mistress Juno and her peacocks, as represented by fresco in the doorway of a Lima palace—Calle Ayachucho.

The old unfinished church and deserted monastery of San Francisco de Paula—Calle Malambo.

LOCOMOTION IN SOUTH AMERICA.

What the country people would do down there, if the jackasses were only long enough.
—What they *do* do, is but slightly caricatured by Our Artist.

Ladies' style as seen at the theatre.

Also Our Artist before and after he had his hair cut in the latest Lima fashion.

A FRUIT-STALL AT CHORRILLOS.

Our Artist, as he appeared when stricken with amazement at the huge clusters of white grapes that are everywhere, for a mere song, sold in Peru.

SHOPPING IN PERU.

A Peruvian materfamilias, having bought a few simple house-keeping articles in town, is here seen returning to her mountain home, accompanied by her purchases.

37

Having been nearly devoured by these carnivorous little devils, Our Artist sprinkles himself with Turkish flea-powder one night before retiring, and is charmed at the rapid and parabolic manner with which they desert him.

38

THE LLAMAS OF PERU.

Our Artist had heretofore fancied that it would be immensely jolly to ride one of these singular beasts of burden ; but when he encounters this one, on a lonely road outside the walls one day, he begs to be excused.

39

Our Artist assists at a mask-ball in the Jardin Otaiza, and is puzzled at the nationality of the costumes worn by the dancers.

CHURCH ORNAMENTS IN LIMA.

The statues in the niches and on the spires of the Cathedral look very well in the daytime; but at night, when the turkey-buzzards roost on their heads, the solemnity of the thing is some. what marred.

41

Lima is full of churches, and the churches are full of bells ; and as they ring and bang away from dewy eve till early morn, their cadences are calculated to disturb somewhat the peaceful slumbers of Our Artist.

42

PERUVIAN BARK—IN THE ROUGH.

Our Artist is treated to plenty of this quinine (canine) salutation, whenever and wherever he pays a visit in Lima.

43

"This pig went to market," but as. he wouldn't go decently, he was tied upon the back of the ever-patient donkey, and so, *nolens volens*, came to Lima, crossing the bridge over the Rimac, where Our Artist sketched him.

A theological discussion of the gravest import takes place between three jolly Fathers of the Roman Catholic Church—a Dominican, a Mercedarian, and a Buena-Muertean.

Scene—The square in front of the church of San Francisco, with its crooked cross.

Our Artist doesn't want to say anything against the insects of Peru; but the way in which one of his hands swelled up, after a bite from some unknown varmit in the night, was, to say the least, alarming.

LOTTERIES IN PERU.

Having invested in the semi-monthly Lima lottery, Our Artist feels so confident of drawing the $4,000 prize, that he gets extravagant, wears his good clothes, and smokes one-dollar cigars; but a revulsion of feeling takes place after the drawing produces nothing for him but blanks.

47

Having been informed by a musty old sepulchral monk that the remains of Pizarro might be seen behind this grating, Our Artist tremblingly gazes therein—but as it is pitch dark, he doesn't recognize Pizarro.

A COUP D'ŒIL IN LIMA.

A picturesque view of the great stone bridge over the rapid river Rimac, showing the towers of the church Desamparados, the Arch with illuminated clock, and the spire of Santo Domingo. —Sketched with about ninety-seven Peruvian beggars looking over Our Artist's shoulder.

A visit to the Museum—which contains a not very remarkable collection of Peruvian antiquities—and where Our Artist sees all that remains of the once magnificent Atahualpa, last king of the Incas.

Alas, poor Yorick ! To this complexion must we come at last.—Fit sketch wherewith to end this strange, eventful history of " Our Artist in Peru."

www.ingramcontent.com/pod-product-compliance
Lightning Source LLC
Chambersburg PA
CBHW031757090426
42739CB00008B/1053